Frank and a Dog Named Pup

Written by Pauline Hensley Harber

Illustrated by Barbara Rochelle Wills

An Ascended Ideas original

Ascended Ideas Publishing
http://www.ascendedideas.com

ISBN:979-8-218-98254-6

Cover and interior art by Barbara Rochelle Wills

Printed in the United States of America

Many, many years ago deep in the beautiful mountains of Harlan, Kentucky where clear rippling streams flowed to the valley, there was once a little shack. It sat at the foot of the mountain in School House Hollow which was in Martins Fork. It was there that a little nine year old boy lived. His name was Frank.

Frank's dad died when he was two leaving behind Frank, his sister, Mary Ruth; his brothers, Willard, Esco, and Sam; and his momma, Liddie. Times were hard for a widow woman in the mountains of Harlan County back in the 1940s.

Frank and his momma walked across the mountain every month to the post office that sat at the end of the hollow on the other side of the mountain. It was there that they picked up the meager check that they received because Frank's dad had been a coal miner.

One beautiful autumn day as they made their journey back from the post office, Liddie and Frank stopped in the hollow to chat with Saul, Betsy and their children. They were a fine African American family who came to the area for Saul to work in the coal mines.

As Liddie and Betsy chatted, Frank's eyes lit upon a litter of pups. Frank spotted a little white pup with a couple of large black spots covering more than half his head and face.

Saul could see that Frank and the puppy were best friends at that very moment. Frank called out "Momma, can I take this one home with me?"

Liddie softly replied, "Frank, Saul might not want to give it away."

To Frank's delight, Saul said, "Now, Liddie, one man only needs so many dogs...Frank can have the one he holds."

Frank cried out, half laughter and half tears, "Oh, thank you, thank you, Saul."

Frank carried the little puppy across the colorful mountain believing that the puppy would be his best friend. He had been a lonely child; he sat in the mountains many times and just cried. Now he knew he would never be alone again.

"Momma," he cried out as he was tired and a little behind. "I am going to call him Pup, Pup will be his name."

As that year passed, Frank and Pup roamed the mountains together watching the hawks sail as they enjoyed the quiet mountain life. When Pup sensed that Frank was lonely, he sat close to him and lay his head in Frank's lap.

Frank and Pup hunted wild game to put food on the table; this made his momma very proud of her little man.

One day Frank's momma took sick and not many weeks after she went to Heaven. Frank was now ten years old and an orphan. As he sat in the woods weeping that day, Pup stayed by his side.

After his momma's funeral, for some unknown reason, a relative took Frank's pup away to a valley that was below the post office on the other side of the mountain.

Frank, his sister and his brothers went to live with their Aunt Ruthie and Uncle Henry, and their two sons and two daughters. They loaded their few belongings on an old flatbed truck and drove out of School House Hollow, leaving their little shack behind.

Their new home sat on a hill and was less than two miles from School House Hollow. The little white house had porches with white banisters across the front and back.

With only two bedrooms, the six boys shared one bedroom with wall to wall beds. At night Frank's mind covered the many days when he and Pup roamed the mountains together when his momma was alive.

Frank had no idea that Pup was on his way home. Pup traveled many miles up the highway, hollow, and through the mountains, crossing streams and moving through thick undergrowth.

He first came to the little shack in School House Hollow to find everyone gone. He followed his best friend's scent down the hollow and up the road that led to Frank's new home.

It was a cold wintery night when Frank was awakened by a sad howl. He yelled to the other five boys, "Do you hear a dog howling?"

Sam, shouted, "Sounds like Pup to me!" They jumped out of their beds running to the front porch, wearing only their long johns.

Their world was lit up by the full moon. Frank spotted Pup at the bottom of the hill. The boys all danced with glee as Frank ran to meet Pup and held him, whining a happy whine right along with Pup.

As Frank lay in bed, holding Pup close, he knew that God had led his Pup home because He knew it would be too hard for a little mountain boy to lose his momma and best friend, too.

The little orphan boy and his little dog Pup spent many years exploring the mountains, watching the hawks sail again and the squirrels storing hickory nuts for winter. They just enjoyed their lives together, not worrying about survival.

Pup could hear the sound of the school bus that Frank rode and knew long before it rounded the curve that Frank was almost home. When Frank's chores were done, Pup headed for the mountains knowing Frank would be behind him. Frank and Pup were able to spend ten more years playing and hunting in the mountains that were dear to their hearts.

Frank grew up and Pup went to Dog Heaven. At nineteen, Frank left the mountains and went north to Illinois to work in the city, but he carried his memories with him.
Frank worked very hard and one day became a very wealthy man. The fear of being without made him a hard worker.

That little boy that was orphaned in 1949 is now an older man, but he visits his beloved mountains every summer and takes early morning strolls to the places where he and Pup roamed the hills and mountains long ago. To him it seems like only yesterday as his memories live on.

The End

About the Author

Pauline Hensley Harber is the author of Among the Mountain Laurels as well as Echoes from the Mountains. Her upcoming novel Mountain Destiny should be released in late 2010 or early 2011. She is a retired Sociology and Psychology teacher and lives in Smith, KY with her husband.

[mountainlaurel@kymail.com]

About the Artist

Kentucky artist Barbara Rochelle Wills, originally from Jeffersontown, now calls the beautiful Appalachian mountains of the southeastern corner of the state her home. There in her Harlan County studio near the small town of Loyall, she lives and creates her works of art. Barbara received her education at Morehead State University, and she continues her training in nationally acclaimed workshops.

Contact Information:

Barbara Rochelle Wills
Studio of Fine Art and Portraiture
P.O. Box 604, Loyall, KY 40854
(606) 273-2585 brwillsart@hotmail.com

Author Dedications

Especially for Frank and Ruby Twinam, their daughter Donna, grandchildren: T.J., Aaron, Sam, & Sarah Gerhart; and great grandson Alexzander Dean Rhodenbaugh.

My dad's great, great nephew, Brady Hensley Robison.

Great nephews and nieces:

Hunter & John Beard.

Ben, Jenna, & Matthew Hoskins.

Colin & Kyle Bargo.

Lydia, Jackie, and Russ Hensley.

Great Grandson, Malachi Scroggins.

And a special, little friend, Alyssa Gibson.

Thanks

A special thanks to Rhonda Robinson for her unending support.